SING AS WE GO

Edited by Helen Exley

EXLEY

To Little Song,

who knows exactly who he is
and where he's going

Always sing as you go!

Published in Great Britain in 1986 by
Exley Publications Ltd
16 Chalk Hill, Watford, Herts WD1 4BN, United Kingdom.
Reprinted 1987
Reprinted 1992

British Library Cataloguing in Publication Data
Sing as we go.
　　1.　Children's songs, English — Texts.
　　I.　Exley, Helen.
　　784.6'2405　　　　PZ8.3

ISBN 1-85015-044-3 (h/b)
ISBN 1-85015-043-5 (p/b)

Front cover illustration by Mike Scott.
Illustrations by Dalton Exley, Sacha Gilchrist and Mike Scott.
Designed by Nick Maddren.
Typeset by Brush Off Studios, St Albans, Herts.
Printed and bound in Hungary.

Introduction

Every journey goes more quickly, goes more happily with a song. It makes a holiday or outing enjoyable right from the start. Unfortunately – if you're like my family – there's usually a bit of a problem with the words. You can't remember them; you haven't a clue about the second verse; and you completely forget about the song you so much wanted to share with everybody. With *Sing as we go* I hope you'll have the solution. Flick through the pages and I bet you'll spot ten real old favourites right away.

Hopefully the book will lead to a few more smiles on long journeys. Grumpy dads and tense drivers will relax a bit. The miles will disappear, and even the sulkies in the back will join in. It's been great fun preparing the book. I had the help of Little Song, a special member of my family who insists on anonymity. As a child, he sang everywhere. Even his teachers complained. Then there was an *awful silence* for several years. But now he's rather large, he's started to sing again and once again I know how important singing is in our lives. So together we collected these favourites.

I hope you like them. Have fun. And remember – it doesn't matter a hoot if you're out of tune as long as you sing LOUDLY!

Helen Exley

Contents

London Bridge is falling down

London Bridge is falling down ,
   Falling down, falling down,
London Bridge is falling down,
   My fair lady.

How shall we build it up again,
   Up again, up again,
How shall we build it up again,
   My fair lady?

Build it up with silver and gold
   Silver and gold, silver and gold,
Build it up with silver and gold,
   My fair lady.

Silver and gold will be stolen away,
   Stolen away, stolen away,
Silver and gold will be stolen away,
   My fair lady.

Build it up with wood and clay,
   Wood and clay, wood and clay,
Build it up with wood and clay.,
   My fair lady.

Wood and clay will wash away,
   Wash away, wash away,
Wood and clay will wash away,
   My fair lady.

Build it up with iron and steel,
Iron and steel, iron and steel,
Build it up with iron and steel,
My fair lady.

Iron and steel will bend and bow,
Bend and bow, bend and bow,
Iron and steel will bend and bow,
My fair lady.

Build it up with stone so strong,
Stone so strong, stone so strong,
Build it up with stone so strong,
My fair lady.

Stone will last for ages long,
Ages long, ages long,
Stone will last for ages long,
My fair lady.

Dance to your daddy

Dance to your daddy,
my little laddie,
Dance to your daddy,
my little man.
You shall have a fishy
on a little dishy.
You shall have a fishy
when the boat comes in.
Dance to your daddy,
my little laddie,
Dance to your daddy,
my little man.

London's burning

Traditional

London's burning; London's burning,
Fetch the engines, fetch the engines;
Fire! Fire! Fire! Fire!
Pour on water, pour on water.
(Repeat as a round)

Three blind mice

Three blind mice,
Three blind mice,
See how they run!
See how they run!
They all ran after the farmer's wife,
Who cut off their tails with a carving knife,
Did you ever see such a thing in your life
As three blind mice?

Froggie went a-courtin'

Froggie went a-courtin' and he did ride, a-huh, a-huh,
Froggie went a-courtin' and he did ride,
Sword and pistol by his side, a-huh, a-huh.

Well, he rode down to Miss Mouse's door, a-huh, a-huh,
Well, he rode down to Miss Mouse's door,
Where he had often been before, a-huh, a-huh.

He took Miss Mousie on his knee, a-huh, a-huh,
He took Miss Mousie on his knee,
Said 'Miss Mousie will you marry me?' a-huh, a-huh.

'I'll have to ask my Uncle Rat' a-huh, a-huh,
'I'll have to ask my Uncle Rat,
'See what he will say to that' a-huh, a-huh.

'Without my Uncle Rat's consent' a-huh, a-huh,
'Without my Uncle Rat's consent
I would not marry the President.' a-huh, a-huh.

Well, Uncle Rat laughed and shook his fat sides, a-huh, a-huh,
Well, Uncle Rat laughed and shook his fat sides,
To think his niece would be a bride, a-huh, a-huh.

Well, Uncle Rat rode off to town, a-huh, a-huh,
Well, Uncle Rat rode off to town,
To buy his niece a wedding gown, a-huh, a-huh.

'Where will the wedding supper be?' a-huh, a-huh,
'Where will the wedding supper be?'
'Way down yonder in a hollow tree.' a-huh, a-huh.

'What will the wedding supper be?' a-huh, a-huh,
'What will the wedding supper be?'
'A fried mosquito and a roasted flea.' a-huh, a-huh.

First to come in were two little ants, a-huh, a-huh,
First to come in were two little ants,
Fixing around to have a dance, a-huh, a-huh.

Next to come in was a bumble bee, a-huh, a-huh,
Next to come in was a bumble bee,
Bouncing a fiddle on his knee, a-huh, a-huh.

Next to come in was a fat sassy lad, a-huh, a-huh,
Next to come in was a fat sassy lad,
Thinks himself as big as his dad, a-huh, a-huh.

Thinks himself a man indeed, a-huh, a-huh,
Thinks himself a man indeed,
Because he chews the tobacco weed, a-huh, a-huh.

And next to come in was a big tomcat, a-huh, a-huh,
And next to come in was a big tomcat,
He swallowed the frog and the mouse and the rat, a-huh, a-huh.

Next to come in was a big old snake, a-huh, a-huh,
Next to come in was a big old snake,
He chased the party into the lake, a-huh, a-huh.

sassy: saucy

The grand old Duke of York

Oh, the grand old Duke of York,
He had ten thousand men;
He marched them up to the top of the hill
And he marched them down again.

And when they were up, they were up;
And when they were down, they were down;
And when they were only half way up,
They were neither up nor down.

The runaway train

Words by Robert E. Massey

The runaway train came down the track
    And she blew, she blew.
The runaway train came down the track
    And she blew, she blew.
The runaway train came down the track,
Her whistle wide and her throttle back,
    And she blew, blew, blew, blew, blew.

The engineer said the train must halt,
    And she blew, she blew.
The engineer said the train must halt,
    And she blew, she blew.
The engineer said the train must halt,
He said it was all the fireman's fault,
    And she blew, blew, blew, blew, blew.

The fireman said he rang the bell,
    And she blew, she blew.
The fireman said he rang the bell,
    And she blew, she blew.
The fireman said he rang the bell,
The engineer said 'You did like hell!'
    And she blew, blew, blew, blew, blew.

The runaway train went over the hill,
    And she blew, she blew.
The runaway train went over the hill,
    And she blew, she blew.
The runaway train went over the hill,
And the last we heard she was going still,
    And she blew, blew, blew, blew, blew.

Old MacDonald had a farm

Old MacDonald had a farm,
Ee-i, ee-i, Oh!
And on this farm he had some chicks,
Ee-i, ee-i, Oh!
With a chick chick here
And a chick chick there,
Here a chick, there a chick,
Everywhere a chick chick,
Old MacDonald had a farm,
Ee-i, ee-i, Oh!

Old MacDonald had a farm,
Ee-i, ee-i, Oh!
And on this farm he had some ducks,
Ee-i, ee-i, Oh!
With a quack quack here
And a quack quack there,
Here a quack, there a quack,
Everywhere a quack quack,
Old MacDonald had a farm,
Ee-i, ee-i, Oh!

Old MacDonald had a farm,
Ee-i, ee-i, Oh!
And on this farm he had some dogs,
Ee-i, ee-i, Oh!
With a bow wow here

And a bow wow there,
Here a bow wow, there a bow wow,
Everywhere a bow wow,
Old MacDonald had a farm,
Ee-i, ee-i, Oh!

Old MacDonald had a farm,
Ee-i, ee-i, Oh!
And on this farm he had some cows,
Ee-i, ee-i, Oh!
With a moo moo here,
And a moo moo there,
Here a moo, there a moo,
Everywhere a moo moo,
Old MacDonald had a farm,
Ee-i, ee-i, Oh!

Old MacDonald had a farm,
Ee-i, ee-i, Oh!
And on this farm he had some pigs,
Ee-i, ee-i, Oh!
With an oink oink here,
And an oink oink there,
Here an oink, there an oink,
Everywhere an oink oink,
Old MacDonald had a farm,
Ee-i, ee-i, Oh!

Go tell Aunt Rhody

Go tell Aunt Rhody,
Go tell Aunt Rhody,
Go tell Aunt Rhody,
The old grey goose is dead –

The one that she's been fattening,
The one that she's been fattening,
The one that she's been fattening,
To make a feather bed.

She died last Thursday,
(Repeat twice)
A sore pain in her head.

The old gander's mourning,
(Repeat twice)
Because his wife is dead.

The goslings are weeping,
(Repeat twice)
Because they've not been fed.

We'll have a funeral,
(Repeat twice)
Is what the parson said.

She'll have a tombstone
(Repeat twice)
To stand above her head.

And by the graveside,
(Repeat twice)
We'll plant some roses red.

The blue-tail fly

When I was young I used to wait
On master and give him his plate,
And pass the bottle when he got dry,
And brush away the blue-tail fly.

Chorus:
Jimmy crack corn and I don't care,
Jimmy crack corn and I don't care,
Jimmy crack corn and I don't care,
My master's gone away.

When he rode in the afternoon
I'd follow him with hick'ry broom,
The pony, being rather shy
When bitten by the blue-tail fly.
(Chorus)

Once when he rode around the farm
The flies about him thick did swarm,
The pony which was very shy
Was bitten by the blue-tail fly.
(Chorus)

The pony run, he jump, he pitch,
He throw my master in a ditch;
He died and the jury wondered why;
The verdict was, "The blue-tail fly!"
    (Chorus)

They laid him 'neath a 'simmon tree,
His epitaph is there to see:
"Beneath this stone I'm forced to lie,
A victim of the blue-tail fly."
    (Chorus)

Row, row, row your boat

Row, row, row your boat,
Gently down the stream,
Merrily, merrily, merrily, merrily,
Life is but a dream.

Pop goes the weasel

All around the cobbler's bench ,
The monkey chased the weasel.
The monkey thought 'twas all in fun,
Pop goes the weasel!
I've no time to wait and sigh,
No patience to wait till by 'n by,
So kiss me quick, I'm off, goodbye,
Pop goes the weasel!

A nickel for a spool of thread,
A penny for a needle,
That's the way the money goes,
Pop goes the weasel!
You may try to sew and sew,
And never make something regal,
So roll it up and let it go,
Pop goes the weasel!

I went to a lawyer today,
For something very legal,
He asked how much I'm willing to pay –
Pop goes the weasel!
I will bargain all my days,
But never again so feeble,
I paid for ev'ry legal phrase,
Pop goes the weasel!

A painter would his lover to paint,
He stood before the easel,
A monkey jumped all over the paint,
Pop goes the weasel!
When his lover she did laugh,
His temper got very lethal,
He tore the painting up in half,
Pop goes the weasel!

I went up and down on the coast,
To find a golden eagle,
I climbed the rocks and thought I was close,
Pop goes the weasel!
But, alas! I lost my way,
Saw nothing but just a sea gull,
I tore my pants and killed the day,
Pop goes the weasel!

I went to a grocery store,
I thought a little cheese'll
Be good to catch a mouse in the floor,
Pop goes the weasel!
But the mouse was very bright,
He wasn't a mouse to wheedle,
He took the cheese and said "goodnight",
Pop goes the weasel!

I went hunting up in the woods,
It wasn't very legal,
The dog and I were caught with the goods,
Pop goes the weasel!
I said I didn't hunt or sport,
The warden looked at my beagle,
He said to tell it to the court,
Pop goes the weasel!

My son and I we went to the fair,
And there were lots of people,
We spent a lot of money, I swear,
Pop goes the weasel!
I got sick from all the sun,
My sonny boy got the measles,
But still we had a lot of fun,
Pop goes the weasel!

The big rock candy mountain

Traditional American hobo song

Chorus:
Oh, the buzzing of the bees
In the cigarette trees
And the soda water fountain,
By the lemonade springs
  where the bluebird sings
In the big rock candy mountain!

On a warm spring day in the month of May,
A burly bum came hiking
Down a shady lane near the sugar cane.
He was looking for his liking.
As he strolled along, he sang a song
Of a land of milk and honey
Where a bum can stay for many a day,
And he won't need any money.
  (Chorus)

In the big rock candy mountain,
All the cops have wooden legs.
The bulldogs all have rubber teeth
And the hens lay soft-boiled eggs.
The farmers' trees are full of fruit,
And the barns are full of hay.
Oh, I want to go where there ain't no snow,
Where the sleet don't fall
  and the rain don't blow,
In the big rock candy mountain!
  (Chorus)

In the big rock candy mountain,
You need never change your socks.
And fizzy streams of fine champagne
Come trickling down the rocks.
The boxcars all are empty,
And the railroad bulls are blind.
There's a lake of stew and ginger ale too.
You can paddle all 'round in a big canoe,
In the big rock candy mountain.
  (Chorus)

In the big rock candy mountain,
All the jails are made of tin,
And you can break right out again
As soon as they throw you in.

bum: tramp
railroad bull: railway policeman

The Hippopotamus

Words by Michael Flanders

A bold Hippopotamus was standing one day
On the banks of the cool Shalimar.
He gazed at the bottom as it peacefully lay
By the light of the evening star.
Away on the hill top sat combing her hair
His fair Hippopotamine maid.
The Hippopotamus
Was no ignoramus
And sang her this sweet serenade.

Chorus:
Mud! Mud! Glorious mud!
Nothing quite like it for cooling the blood.
So, follow me, follow, down to the hollow,
And there let us wallow in Glorious mud.

The fair Hippopotama he aimed to entice
From her seat on the hill top above
As she hadn't got a ma to give her advice
Came tiptoeing down to her love.
Like thunder the forest re-echoed the sound
Of the song that they sang as they met
His inamorata
Adjusted her garter
And lifted her voice in duet.
    (Chorus)

Now more Hippopotami began to convene
On the banks of that river so wide.
I wonder now what am I to say of the scene
That ensued by the Shalimar side.
They dived all at once with an ear-splitting
    splosh,
Then rose to the surface again.
A regular army
Of Hippopotami
All singing this haunting refrain.
    (Chorus)

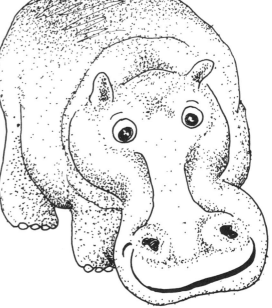

One man went to mow

Traditional

One man went to mow,
Went to mow a meadow,
One man and his dog,
Went to mow a meadow.

Two men went to mow,
Went to mow a meadow,
Two men, one man and his dog,
Went to mow a meadow.

Three men went to mow,
Went to mow a meadow,
Three men, two men, one man and his dog,
Went to mow a meadow.

Four men went to mow,
Went to mow a meadow,
Four men, three men, two men, one man
  and his dog,
Went to mow a meadow.

Five men went to mow,
Went to mow a meadow,
Five men, four men, three men, two men,
  one man and his dog,
Went to mow a meadow.

Six men went to mow,
Went to mow a meadow,
Six men, five men, four men, three men, two men, one man
    and his dog,
Went to mow a meadow.

Seven men went to mow,
Went to mow a meadow,
Seven men, six men, five men, four men, three men, two men,
    one man and his dog,
Went to mow a meadow.

Eight men went to mow,
Went to mow a meadow,
Eight men, seven men, six men, five men, four men, three men,
    two men, one man and his dog,
Went to mow a meadow.

Nine men went to mow,
Went to mow a meadow,
Nine men, eight men, seven men, six men, five men, four men,
    three men, two men, one man and his dog,
Went to mow a meadow.

Ten men went to mow,
Went to mow a meadow,
Ten men, nine men, eight men, seven men, six men, five men,
    four men, three men, two men, one man and his dog,
Went to mow a meadow.

If you're happy

Traditional American

If you're happy and you know it,
    Clap your hands.
If you're happy and you know it,
    Clap your hands.
If you're happy and you know it,
Then you'll surely want to show it,
If you're happy and you know it,
    Clap your hands.

If you're happy and you know it,
    nod your head.
If you're happy and you know it,
    nod your head.
If you're happy and you know it,
Then you'll surely want to show it,
If you're happy and you know it,
    nod your head.

If you're happy and you know it,
    stamp your feet.
If you're happy and you know it,
    stamp your feet.
If you're happy and you know it,
Then you'll surely want to show it,
If you're happy and you know it,
    stamp your feet.

If you're happy and you know it,
    say 'Ha! Ha!'
If you're happy and you know it,
    say 'Ha! Ha!'
If you're happy and you know it,
Then you'll surely want to show it,
If you're happy and you know it,
    say 'Ha! Ha!'

If you're happy and you know it,
    do all four!
If you're happy and you know it,
    do all four!
If you're happy and you know it,
Then you'll surely want to show it,
If you're happy and you know it,
    do all four!

Ten in the bed

Traditional

There were ten in the bed
And the little one said,
'Roll over! Roll over'
So they all rolled over and one fell out.

There were nine in the bed
(Repeat, as in first verse)

There were eight in the bed
(Repeat as in first verse)

There were seven in the bed
(Repeat, as in first verse)

There were six in the bed
(Repeat, as in first verse)

There were five in the bed
(Repeat, as in first verse)

There were four in the bed
(Repeat, as in first verse)

There were three in the bed
(Repeat, as in first verse)

There were two in the bed
(Repeat, as in first verse)

There was one in the bed
And this little one said,
'Good night! Good night!'

There's a hole in my bucket

Traditional

There's a hole in my bucket, dear Liza, dear Liza,
There's a hole in my bucket, dear Liza, a hole.

Then mend it, dear Georgie, dear Georgie, dear Georgie,
Then mend it, dear Georgie, dear Georgie, mend it!

With what shall I mend it, dear Liza, dear Liza?
With what shall I mend it, dear Liza, with what?

With a straw, dear Georgie, dear Georgie, dear Georgie,
With a straw, dear Georgie, dear Georgie, a straw!

The straw is too long, dear Liza, dear Liza,
The straw is too long, dear Liza, too long.

Then cut it, dear Georgie, dear Georgie, dear Georgie,
Then cut it, dear Georgie, dear Georgie, cut it!

With what shall I cut it, dear Liza, dear Liza?
With what shall I cut it, dear Liza, with what?

With a knife, dear Georgie, dear Georgie, dear Georgie,
With a knife, dear Georgie, dear Georgie, a knife!

The knife is too blunt, dear Liza, dear Liza,
The knife is too blunt, dear Liza, too blunt.

Then sharpen it, dear Georgie, dear Georgie, dear Georgie,
Then sharpen it, dear Georgie, dear Georgie, sharpen it!

With what shall I sharpen it, dear Liza, dear Liza?
With what shall I sharpen it, dear Liza, with what?

With a stone, dear Georgie, dear Georgie, dear Georgie,
With a stone, dear Georgie, dear Georgie, a stone!

The stone is too dry, dear Liza, dear Liza,
The stone is too dry, dear Liza, too dry.

Then wet it, dear Georgie, dear Georgie, dear Georgie,
Then wet it, dear Georgie, dear Georgie, wet it!

With what shall I wet it, dear Liza, dear Liza?
With what shall I wet it, dear Liza, with what?

With water, dear Georgie, dear Georgie, dear Georgie,
With water, dear Georgie, dear Georgie, with water!

In what shall I get it, dear Liza, dear Liza?
In what shall I get it, dear Liza, in what?

In a bucket, dear Georgie, dear Georgie, dear Georgie,
In a bucket, dear Georgie, dear Georgie, in a bucket!

There's a hole in my bucket, dear Liza, dear Liza,
There's a hole in my bucket, dear Liza, a hole.

Cock-a-doodle -doo!

Cock-a-doodle-doo!
My dame has lost her shoe,
My master's lost his fiddling stick
And doesn't know what to do.

Cock-a-doodle-doo!
What is my dame to do?
Till master finds his fiddling stick
She'll dance without her shoe.

Cock-a-doodle-doo!
My dame has found her shoe,
And master's found his fiddling stick,
Sing doodle-doodle-doo.

Cock-a-doodle-doo!
My dame will dance with you,
While master fiddles his fiddling stick
For dame and doodle-doo.

Ring-a-ring o' roses

Ring-a-ring o' roses,
A pocket full of posies.
A-tishoo! A-tishoo!
We'll all fall down.

The king has sent his daughter
To fetch a pail of water.
A-tishoo! A-tishoo!
We'll all fall down.

The bird upon the steeple
Sits high above the people.
A-tishoo! A-tishoo!
We'll all fall down.

The wedding bells are ringing,
The boys and girls are singing.
A-tishoo! A-tishoo!
We'll all fall down.

The Quartermaster's stores

Traditional army song

There were rats, rats,
Big as bloomin' cats,
In the stores, in the stores,
There were rats, rats,
Lying about on mats,
In the Quartermaster's stores.

Chorus:
My eyes are dim, I cannot see,
I have not brought my specs with me,
I have not brought my specs with me.

There was steak, steak,
Tough as cattle cake,
In the stores, in the stores,
There was steak, steak,
To give you belly ache,
In the Quartermaster's stores.
(Chorus)

There was bread, bread,
Harder than your head,
In the stores, in the stores,
There was bread, bread,
Just like lumps of lead,
In the Quartermaster's stores.
(Chorus)

She'll be comin' 'round the mountain

Traditional American railroad song

She'll be comin' 'round the mountain
When she comes.
She'll be comin' 'round the mountain
When she comes.
She'll be comin' 'round the mountain.
She'll be comin' 'round the mountain.
She'll be comin' 'round the mountain
When she comes.

She'll be driving six white horses
When she comes.
(Repeat, as in first verse)

She'll be shining bright as silver
When she comes.
(Repeat, as in first verse)

She will neither rock nor totter
When she comes.
(Repeat, as in first verse)

Oh, we'll all go out to meet her
When she comes.
(Repeat, as in first verse)

We will kill the old red rooster
When she comes.
(Repeat, as in first verse)

And we'll all have chicken and dumplings
When she comes.
(Repeat, as in first verse)

There'll be joy and smiles and laughter
When she comes.
(Repeat, as in first verse)

But it may be just a while yet
'Fore she comes.
Yes, it may be just a while yet
'Fore she comes.
Oh, it may be just a while yet,
Yes, it may be just a while yet,
And it may be just a while yet
'Fore she comes.

Drink to me only with thine eyes

Drink to me only with thine eyes,
And I will pledge with mine;
Or leave a kiss within the cup,
And I'll not ask for wine.
The thirst that from the soul doth rise,
Doth ask a drink divine,
But might I of Jove's nectar sip,
I would not change for thine.

I sent thee late a rosy wreath,
Not so much hon'ring thee,
As giving it a hope that there
It could not withered be;
But thou thereon dids't only breathe,
And send'st it back to me,
Since when it grows and smells, I swear,
Not of itself, but thee.

Ten green bottles

Traditional

Ten green bottles hanging on the wall,
Ten green bottles hanging on the wall,
And if one green bottle should accidentally fall,
There'd be nine green bottles hanging on the wall.

Nine green bottles hanging on the wall,
Nine green bottles hanging on the wall,
And if one green bottle should accidentally fall,
There'd be eight green bottles hanging on the wall.

(Repeat for eight, seven, six, five, four, three and two)

One green bottle hanging on the wall,
One green bottle hanging on the wall,
And if that green bottle should accidentally fall,
There'd be no green bottles hanging on the wall.

For he's a jolly good fellow

For he's a jolly good fellow,
For he's a jolly good fellow,
For he's a jolly good fellow,
Which nobody can deny!

We won't go home until morning,
We won't go home until morning,
We won't go home until morning,
Till daylight doth appear!

The bear went over the mountain,
The bear went over the mountain,
The bear went over the mountain,
To see what he could see!
   (Yell)
   And all that he could see was

The other side of the mountain,
The other side of the mountain,
The other side of the mountain,
Was all that he could see!

This old man

Traditional English counting rhyme

This old man, he plays One.
He plays nick-nack
  on my thumb.

Chorus:
With a nick-nack,
Paddy-whack,
Give the dog a bone,
This old man goes rolling home.

This old man, he plays Two.
He plays nick-nack
  on my shoe.
    (Chorus)

This old man, he plays Three.
He plays nick-nack
  on my knee.
    (Chorus)

This old man, he plays Four.
He plays nick-nack
  on my door.
    (Chorus)

This old man, he plays Five.
He plays nick-nack
  on my hive.
    (Chorus)

This old man, he plays Six.
He plays nick-nack
  on my sticks.
    (Chorus)

This old man, he plays Seven.
Cross my heart and
  go to Heaven.
    (Chorus)

This old man, he plays Eight.
He plays nick-nack
  on my gate.
    (Chorus)

This old man, he plays Nine.
He plays nick-nack
  on my twine.
    (Chorus)

This old man, he plays Ten.
He plays nick-nack
  with his friends.
    (Chorus)

This old man, he plays 'Leven.
He plays nick-nack
  four and seven.
    (Chorus)

This old man, he plays Twelve.
He plays nick-nack
  by himself
    (Chorus)

This old man, he plays Teens.
He plays nick-nack
  with string beans.
    (Chorus)

This old man, he plays Twenty.
He plays nick-nack
  on my pennies.
    (Chorus)

Day trip to Bangor

Words & music by Debbie Cook

Chorus:
Didn't we have a lovely time the day we went to Bangor,
a beautiful day, we had lunch on the way
and all for under a pound, you know
that on the way back I cuddled with Jack
and we opened a bottle of cider,
Singing a few of our favourite songs
   As the wheels went round.

Do you recall the thrill of it all
as we walked along the sea-front?
Then on the sand we heard a brass band
that played the Tidd-ley-pom-te-ra-ra.
Elsie and me had one cuppa tea
then we took a ped-a-lo boat out.
Splashing away as we sailed round the bay
   As the wheels went round.
      (Chorus)

Wasn't it nice eating chocolate ice
as we strolled around the fun-fair?
Then we ate eels on the Big Ferris Wheel,
we sailed above the ground but then
we had to be quick 'cos Elsie felt sick
and we 'ad to find somewhere to take her.
I said to her lad what made her feel bad
   Was the wheel going round.
      (Chorus)

Elsie and me, we finished our tea
and said goodbye to the seaside.
Climbed on the bus, Flo said to us,
'Oh, isn't it a shame to go?'
Wouldn't it be grand to 'ave cash on demand
and to live like this for always?
It makes me feel ill, when I think on the mill
   And the wheels go round.
   Ya da da dee-dle da da da da dee-dle
   da da da da.

Scarborough Fair

Are you going to Scarborough Fair?
Parsley, sage, rosemary and thyme;
Remember me to one that lives there,
For once she was a true love of mine.

Tell her to make me a cambric shirt,
Parsley, sage, rosemary and thyme;
Without any seam or fine needlework,
And then she'll be a true love of mine.

Tell her to wash it in yonder dry well,
Parsley, sage, rosemary and thyme;
Where water ne'er sprung, nor drop of rain fell,
And then she'll be a true love of mine.

Tell her to dry it on yonder thorn,
Parsley, sage, rosemary and thyme;
Which never bore blossom since Adam was born,
And then she'll be a true love of mine.

Oh, will you find me an acre of land,
Parsley, sage, rosemary and thyme;
Between the sea foam and the sea sand
Or never be a true lover of mine.

Oh, will you plough it with a lamb's horn,
Parsley, sage, rosemary and thyme;
And sow it all over with one peppercorn,
Or never be a true lover of mine.

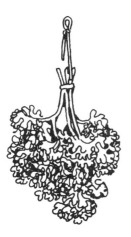

Oh, will you reap it with a sickle of leather,
Parsley, sage, rosemary and thyme;
And tie it all up with a peacock's feather,
Or never be a true lover of mine.

And when you have done and finished your work,
Parsley, sage, rosemary and thyme;
Then come to me for your cambric shirt,
And you shall be a true lover of mine.

Sing as we go

Words & Music by Harry Parr-Davies

Blues, where are you now?
You ought to know that I've no use for you.
Frown, get off my brow.
It's plain to see that from now on we're through.
Turn to the south and sing morning and night,
I see a better day coming in sight.

Chorus:
SING AS WE GO, And let the world go by,
Singing a song we'll march along the highway.
   Say 'Goodbye' to sorrow,
   There's always tomorrow,
   To think of today.

SING AS WE GO, Although the skies are grey,
Beggar or king you've got to sing a gay tune.
A song and a smile making life worth while, so,
SING AS WE GO along.

You'll never regret
The day you say 'On your way' to the clouds.
Take all you can get.
And lift your voice and rejoice while you may.
Happiness comes and goes day after day,
Make up your mind to sing, smile and to say:
   (Chorus)

Going to the zoo

Tom Paxton

Daddy's taking us to the zoo tomorrow
  zoo tomorrow, zoo tomorrow,
Daddy's taking us to the zoo tomorrow.
We can stay all day.

Chorus:
We're going to the zoo, zoo, zoo.
How about you, you, you,
You can come too, too, too.
We're going to the zoo, zoo, zoo.

See the elephant with the long trunk swinging.
  Great big ears and the long trunk swinging
Sniffing up peanuts with the long trunk swinging
We can stay all day.
    (Chorus)

See all the monkeys scrtch, scrtch, scratching
  Jumping all around and scrtch, scrtch, scratching
Hanging by their long tails scrtch, scrtch, scratching
We can stay all day.
    (Chorus)

Big black bear hoov-voo-voo-voofing
  Coat's too heavy, he's hoov-voo-voo-voofing.
Don't get too near hoov-voo-voo-vooting
Or you won't stay all day.
    (Chorus)

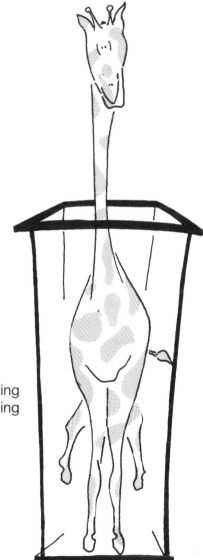

Seals in the pool honk-honk-honking
    Catching fish and honk-honk-honking
Little seals are honk-honk-honking
We can stay all day.
    (Chorus)

Well we stayed all day we're getting sleepy
    Sitting in the car getting sleep, sleep, sleepy
Home already and we're sleep, sleep, sleepy
We have stayed all day.

We've been to the zoo, zoo, zoo.
So have you, you, you.
You came too, too, too.
We've been to the zoo, zoo, zoo.

Momma's taking us to the zoo tomorrow
    zoo tomorrow, zoo tomorrow.
Momma's taking us to the zoo tomorrow.
We can stay all day.
    (Chorus)

Those were the days

Words by Gene Raskin

Once upon a time there was a tavern
Where we used to raise a glass or two.
Remember how we laughed away the hours
And dreamed of all the great things we would do.

Chorus:
Those were the days, my friend,
We thought they'd never end,
We'd sing and dance for ever and a day;
We'd live the life we choose
We'd fight and never lose
For we were young and sure to have our way.
La la la la la la
La la la la la la
Those were the days, oh yes, those were the days.

Then the busy years went rushing by us,
We lost our starry notions on the way.
If by chance I'd see you in the tavern,
We'd smile at one another and we'd say,
    (Chorus)

    Just tonight I stood before the tavern,
    Nothing seemed the way it used to be.
    In the glass I saw a strange reflection,
    Was that lonely woman really me?
        (Chorus)

      Through the door there came familiar laughter,
      I saw your face and heard you call my name.
      Oh my friend we're older but no wiser,
       For in our hearts the dreams are still the same,
          (Chorus)

We shall overcome

Words by Zilphia Horton, Frank Hamilton, Guy Carawan and Pete Seeger

We shall overcome,
We shall overcome,
We shall overcome someday.
Oh, deep in my heart
I do believe,
We shall overcome someday.

We'll walk hand in hand,
We'll walk hand in hand,
We'll walk hand in hand
    someday,
Oh, deep in my heart
I do believe,
We shall overcome someday.

We shall live in peace,
We shall live in peace,
We shall live in peace
    someday,
Oh, deep in my heart
I do believe,
We shall overcome someday.

We shall all be free,
We shall all be free,
We shall all be free someday,
Oh, deep in my heart
I do believe,
We shall overcome someday.

We shall end Jim Crow,
We shall end Jim Crow,
We shall end Jim Crow
    someday,
Oh, deep in my heart
I do believe,
We shall overcome someday.

We are not afraid,
We are not afraid,
We are not afraid today,
Oh, deep in my heart
I do believe,
We shall overcome someday.

The Lord will see us through,
The Lord will see us through,
The Lord will see us through
    someday,
Oh, deep in my heart
I do believe,
We shall overcome someday.

We are not alone,
We are not alone,
We are not alone today,
Oh, deep in my heart
I do believe,
We shall overcome someday.

The whole wide world around,
The whole wide world around,
The whole wide world around
    someday,
Oh, deep in my heart
I do believe,
We shall overcome someday.

We shall overcome,
We shall overcome,
We shall overcome someday,
Oh, deep in my heart
I do believe,
We shall overcome someday.

Where have all the flowers gone?

Words and music by Pete Seeger

Where have all the flowers gone?
Long time passing.
Where have all the flowers gone?
Long time ago.
Where have all the flowers gone?
The girls have picked them ev'ry one.
Oh, when will you ever learn?
Oh, when will you ever learn?

Where have all the young girls gone?
Long time passing.
Where have all the young girls gone?
Long time ago.
Where have all the young girls gone?
They've taken husbands ev'ry one.
Oh, when will you ever learn?
Oh, when will you ever learn?

Where have all the young men gone?
Long time passing.
Where have all the young men gone?
Long time ago.
Where have all the young men gone?
They're all in uniform.
Oh, when will you ever learn?
Oh, when will you ever learn?

Waltzing Matilda

Words by A.B. Paterson

Once a jolly swagman camped by a billabong
Under the shade of a coolibah tree,
And he sang as he watched and waited till his billy boiled,
'You'll come a-waltzing Matilda with me!
  Waltzing Matilda, waltzing Matilda,
  You'll come a-waltzing Matilda with me!'
And he sang as he watched and waited till his billy boiled,
  'You'll come a-waltzing Matilda with me!'

Down came a jumbuck to drink at the billabong,
Up jumped the swagman and grabbed him with glee,
And he sang as he stowed that jumbuck in his tucker-bag,
'You'll come a-waltzing Matilda with me!
  Waltzing Matilda, waltzing Matilda,
  You'll come a-waltzing Matilda with me!'
And he sang as he stowed that jumbuck in his tucker-bag,
  'You'll come a-waltzing Matilda with me!'

Up rode the squatter mounted on his thoroughbred,
Up rode the troopers, one, two, three.
'Where's that jolly jumbuck you've got in your tucker-bag?
'You'll come a-waltzing Matilda with me!
  Waltzing Matilda, waltzing Matilda,
  You'll come a-waltzing Matilda with me!
Where's that jolly jumbuck you've got in your tucker-bag?
  You'll come a-waltzing Matilda with me!'

Up jumped the swagman and sprang into the billabong,
'You'll never take me alive!' said he.
And his ghost may be heard as you pass by that billabong,
'You'll come a-waltzing Matilda with me!
  Waltzing Matilda, waltzing Matilda,
  You'll come a-waltzing Matilda with me!'
And his ghost may be heard as you pass by that billabong,
  'You'll come a-waltzing Matilda with me!'

waltzing Matilda: to travel around looking for work
swagman: travelling worker   billabong: pond
billy: boiling pan   jumbuck: sheep
tucker bag: food bag   squatter: settler

Yankee Doodle

Yankee Doodle went to town,
A-riding on a pony;
Stuck a feather in his hat
And called it macaroni.

Chorus:
Yankee Doodle keep it up,
Yankee Doodle dandy,
Mind the music and the step
And with the girls be handy.

Father and I went down to camp
Along with Captain Gooding;
And there we saw the men and boys,
As thick as hasty pudding.
    (Chorus)

There was Captain Washington,
Upon a slapping stallion,
A-giving orders to his men,
I guess there was a million.
    (Chorus)

macaroni: dandy

Kum ba yah

Kum ba yah, my Lord, Kum ba yah!
Kum ba yah, my Lord, Kum ba yah!
Kum ba yah, my Lord, Kum ba yah!
O Lord, Kum ba yah.

Someone's crying, Lord, Kum ba yah!
Someone's crying, Lord, Kum ba yah!
Someone's crying, Lord, Kum ba yah!
O Lord, Kum ba yah.

Someone's singing, Lord, Kum ba yah!
Someone's singing, Lord, Kum ba yah!
Someone's singing, Lord, Kum ba yah!
O Lord, Kum ba yah.

Someone's praying, Lord, Kum ba yah!
Someone's praying, Lord, Kum ba yah!
Someone's praying, Lord, Kum ba yah!
O Lord, Kum ba yah.

Kookaburra

Traditional Australian

Kookaburra sits in the old gum tree-ee.
Merry, merry king of the bush he-ee.
Laugh, Kookaburra, laugh, Kookaburra,
Gay your life must be.

Kookaburra sits in an old gum tree-ee,
Eating all the gumdrops he can see-ee
Stop, Kookaburra, stop, Kookaburra,
Leave a few for me.

Hava nagila

Traditional Israeli

Hava nagila, hava nagila, hava nagila V' nism'cha.
Hava nagila, hava nagila, hava nagila V' nism'cha.
Hava n'ran'na, hava n'ran'na,
    hava n'ran'na, v' nism'cha.
Hava n'ran'na, hava n'ran'na,
    hava n'ran'na, v' nism'cha.
Uru uru a chim, uru a chim b'lev sameach, uru a chim
    b'lev sameach,
Uru a chim uru a chim b'lev sameach.

Loch Lomond

Traditional Scottish

By yon bonnie banks and by yon bonnie braes
Where the sun shines bright on Loch Lomond,
Where me and my true love were ever wont to be,
On the bonnie, bonnie banks of Loch Lomond.

Chorus:
Oh, you'll take the high road,
And I'll take the low road,
And I'll be in Scotland before you;
But me and my true love will never meet again,
On the bonnie, bonnie banks of Loch Lomond.

braes: hill-slopes

'Twas there that we parted in yon shady glen
On the steep, steep side of Ben Lomond,
Where in purple hue the Highland hills we view,
And the moon coming out in the gloaming.
(Chorus)

The British Grenadiers

Some talk of Alexander and some of Hercules,
Of Hector and Lysander and such great names as these.
But of all the world's brave heroes,
   there's none that can compare
With a tow, row, row, row, row, row,
   to the British Grenadier.

Brown girl in the ring

Traditional Caribbean

There's a brown girl in the ring,
   tra la la la la,
There's a brown girl in the ring,
   tra la la la la,
There's a brown girl in the ring,
   tra la la la la,
For she like sugar and I like plum.

Then you skip across the ocean,
   tra la la la la,
Then you skip across the ocean,
   tra la la la la,
Then you skip across the ocean,
   tra la la la la,
For she like sugar and I like plum.

Then you show me your motion,
   tra la la la la,
Then you show me your motion,
   tra la la la la,
Then you show me your motion,
   tra la la la la,
For she like sugar and I like plum.

Then you wheel an' take your partner,
   tra la la la la,
Then you wheel an' take your partner,
   tra la la la la,
Then you wheel an' take your partner,
   tra la la la la,
For she like sugar and I like plum.

I wish I were in Dixie
(Dixie Land) *Words by Dan Decatur Emmett*

I wish I were in the land of cotton.
Old times they are not forgotten.
    Look away! Look away!
      Look away! Dixie Land.
In Dixie Land where I was born in,
Early on one frosty mornin'.
    Look away! Look away!
      Look away! Dixie Land.

Chorus:
Then I wish I were in Dixie, Hooray! Hooray!
In Dixie Land I'll take my stand,
To live and die in Dixie.
Away, away, away down south in Dixie,
Away, away, away down south in Dixie.

Old Missus married Will the Weaver.
William was a gay deceiver.
    Look away! Look away!
      Look away! Dixie Land.
But when he put his arm around her,
He smiled as fierce as a forty-pounder.
    Look away! Look away!
      Look away! Dixie Land.
      (Chorus)

His face was sharp as a butcher's cleaver,
But that did not seem to grieve her.
    Look away! Look away!
      Look away! Dixie Land.
Old Missus acted the foolish part
And died for a man that broke her heart.
    Look away! Look away!
      Look away! Dixie Land.
      (Chorus)

Now here's a toast to the next old Missus,
And all the girls that want to kiss us.
    Look away! Look away!
        Look away! Dixie Land.
But if you want to drive 'way sorrow.
Come and hear this song tomorrow.
    Look away! Look away!
        Look away! Dixie Land.
        (Chorus)

There's buckwheat cakes and Injun batter,
Makes you fat or a little fatter.
    Look away! Look away!
        Look away! Dixie Land.
Then hoe it down and scratch your gravel.
To Dixie Land I'm bound to travel.
    Look away! Look away!
        Look away! Dixie Land.
        (Chorus)

Gonna cook a meal of grits and 'taters,
Feed what's left to the alligators.
    Look away! Look away!
        Look away! Dixie Land.
And when I die, see that they lay me
'Neath an oak that's cool and shady.
    Look away! Look away!
        Look away! Dixie Land.
        (Chorus)

Camptown Races

Words by Stephen Foster

The Camptown ladies sing this song:
    Doo-dah! Doo-dah!
Camptown racetrack's five miles long.
    Oh! Doo-dah day!
I came down there with my hat caved in.
    Doo-dah! Doo-dah!
I went back home with a pocket full of tin.
    Oh! Doo-dah day!

Chorus:
Going to run all night! Going to run all day!
I'll bet my money on the bobtail nag –
Somebody bet on the bay.

The long-tail filly and the big black horse –
    Doo-dah! Doo-dah!
They fly the track and they both cut across.
    Oh! Doo-dah day!
The blind horse wallowed in a big mud hole –
    Doo-dah! Doo-dah!
Can't touch bottom with a ten-foot pole.
    Oh! Doo-dah day!
      (Chorus)

Old muley cow came onto the track –
    Doo-dah! Doo-dah!
The bobtail flung her over his back.
    Oh! Doo-dah day!
Then flew along like a railroad car
    Doo-dah! Doo-dah!
Running a race with a shooting star.
    Oh! Doo-dah day!
      (Chorus)

See them flying on a ten-mile heat –
    Doo-dah! Doo-dah!
'Round the racetrack, then repeat.
    Oh! Doo-dah day!
I won my money on the bobtail nag.
    Doo-dah! Doo-dah!
I keep my money in an old tow-bag.
    Oh! Doo-dah day!
      (Chorus)

I came from Alabama

Traditional American

I came from Alabama
With my banjo on my knee;
I'm goin' to Louisiana,
My true love for to see.
It rained all night the day I left,
The weather it was dry,
The sun so hot I froze to death,
Susanna, don't you cry.

Chorus:
Oh, Susanna,
Oh, don't you cry for me.
I've come from Alabama
With my banjo on my knee.

I had a dream the other night
When everything was still;
I thought I saw Susanna
A'comin' down the hill.
The buckwheat cake was in her mouth,
A tear was in her eye;
Says I, 'I'm comin' from the South,
Susanna, don't you cry.'
        (Chorus)

Swanee River
(Old folks at home)

Words by Stephen Foster

Way down upon the Swanee River
Far, far away,
That's where my heart is turning ever,
There's where the old folks stay.
All up and down the whole creation
Sadly I roam
Still longing for the old plantation
And for the old folks at home.

Chorus:
All the world is sad and dreary
Everywhere I roam.
Oh, witness how my heart grows weary,
Far from the old folks at home.

All round the little farm I wandered
When I was young.
Then, many happy days I squandered,
Many the songs I sung.
When I was playing with my brother,
Happy was I.
Oh, take me to my kind old mother,
There let me live and die.
    (Chorus)

One little hut among the bushes,
One that I love,
Still sadly to my memory rushes
No matter where I rove.
When will I see the bees a-humming
All 'round the comb?
When will I hear the banjo strumming
Down in my dear old home?
    (Chorus)

Skip to my Lou

Lost my partner what'll I do,
Lost my partner what'll I do,
Lost my partner what'll I do,
Skip to my Lou my darling.

Chorus:
Gone again, skip to my Lou,
Gone again, skip to my Lou,
Gone again, skip to my Lou,
Skip to my Lou my darling.

I'll get another one prettier than you,
I'll get another one prettier than you,
I'll get another one prettier than you,
Skip to my Lou my darling.
    (Chorus)

Little red wagon painted blue,
Little red wagon painted blue,
Little red wagon painted blue,
Skip to my Lou my darling.
    (Chorus)

Flies in the buttermilk two by two,
Flies in the buttermilk two by two,
Flies in the buttermilk two by two,
Skip to my Lou my darling.
    (Chorus)

Flies in the sugar bowl shoo shoo shoo,
Flies in the sugar bowl shoo shoo shoo,
Flies in the sugar bowl shoo shoo shoo,
Skip to my Lou my darling.
    (Chorus)

Going to Texas two by two,
Going to Texas two by two,
Going to Texas two by two,
Skip to my Lou my darling.
    (Chorus)

Cat's in the cream jar what'll I do?
Cat's in the cream jar what'll I do?
Cat's in the cream jar what'll I do?
Skip to my Lou my darling.
    (Chorus)

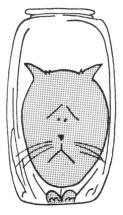

Don't dilly dally on the way

Words by Charles Collins and Fred W. Leigh

My old man said, 'Follow the van,
Don't dilly dally on the way!'
Off went the cart with the home packed in it,
I walked behind with my old cock linnet.
But I dillied and dallied,
Dallied and dillied,
Lost the van and don't know where to roam.
You can't trust the 'specials'
Like the old-time 'coppers'
When you can't find your way home.

Do-re-mi

Words by Oscar Hammerstein II
From the film 'Sound of Music'

Doe, a deer, a female deer,
Ray, a drop of golden sun,
Me, a name I call myself,
Far, a long, long way to run.
Sew, a needle pulling thread,
La, a note to follow sew,
Tea, a drink with jam and bread,
That will bring us back to do oh oh oh!

(Repeat first 7 lines)

That will bring us back to do oh oh oh! doe!
Do re mi fa so la ti do!

Polly-wolly-doodle

O I went down South for to see my Sal,
  Sing Polly-wolly-doodle all the day,
My Sally am a spunky gal,
  Singing Polly-wolly-doodle all the day.

Chorus:
Fare thee well! Fare thee well!
Fare thee well my fairy fay,
O I'm off to Louisiana
For to see my Susy Anna
Singing Polly-wolly-doodle all the day!

O my Sal she am a maiden fair,
  Sing Polly-wolly-doodle all the day
With laughing eyes and curly hair,
  Singing Polly-wolly-doodle all the day.
  (Chorus)

O, a grasshopper sitting on a railway track,
  Sing polly-wolly-doodle all the day
A-picking at his teef wid a carpet tack,
  Singing Polly-wolly-doodle all the day.
  (Chorus)

Behind a barn, down on my knees,
  Sing polly-wolly-doodle all the day
I thought I heard a chicken sneeze,
  Singing Polly-wolly-doodle all the day.
  (Chorus)

He sneezed so hard wid de whooping-cough
  Sing polly-wolly-doodle all the day
He sneezed his head and his tail right off!
  Singing Polly-wolly-doodle all the day.
  (Chorus)

A bicycle built for two (Daisy Bell)

Harry Dacre

There is a flower within my heart, Daisy, Daisy!
Planted one day by a glancing dart,
Planted by Daisy Bell!
Whether she loves me or loves me not,
Sometimes it's hard to tell;
Yet I am longing to share the lot
 of beautiful Daisy Bell!

Chorus:
Daisy, Daisy, give me your answer, do!
I'm half crazy, all for the love of you!
It won't be a stylish marriage,
I can't afford a carriage
But you'll look sweet upon the seat
Of a bicycle built for two.

We will go 'tandem' as man and wife, Daisy, Daisy!
'Peddling' away down the road of life,
I and my Daisy Bell!
When the road's dark we can both despise
P'licemen and 'lamps' as well;
There are 'bright lights' in the dazzling eyes
   of beautiful Daisy Bell!
    (Chorus)

I will stand by you in 'wheel' or woe, Daisy, Daisy!
You'll be the bell(e) which I'll ring, you know!
Sweet little Daisy Bell!
You'll take the 'lead' in each 'trip' we take,
Then, if I don't do well,
I will permit you to use the brake, my beautiful Daisy Bell!
    (Chorus)

It's a long way to Tipperary

First World War song

It's a long way to Tipperary,
It's a long way to go;
It's a long way to Tipperary,
To the sweetest girl I know.
Goodbye, Piccadilly,
Farewell, Leicester Square.
It's a long, long way to Tipperary,
But my heart's right there.

Maybe it's because I'm a Londoner

Words & Music by Hubert Gregg

London isn't everybody's cup of tea,
Often you hear visitors complain
Noisy smoky city but it seems to me
There's magic in the fog and rain.

Chorus:
Maybe it's because I'm a Londoner
That I love London so,
Maybe it's because I'm a Londoner
That I think of her
Wherever I go.
I get a funny feeling inside of me
Just walking up and down,
Maybe it's because I'm a Londoner
That I love London Town.

People take to saying as the years go by,
London isn't London any more
People may be changing but the town and I
We are even closer than before.
    (Chorus)

Jeanie with the light brown hair

Stephen Foster

I dream of Jeanie with the light brown hair,
Borne, like a vapour, on the summer's air;
I see her tripping where the bright streams play,
Happy as the daisies that dance on her way.
Many were the wild notes her merry voice would pour,
Many were the blithe birds that warbled them o'er;
Ah! I dream of Jeanie with the light brown hair,
Floating, like a vapour, on the soft summer air.

I long for Jeanie with the day-dawn smile,
Radiant in gladness, warm with winning guile;
I hear her melodies, like joys gone by,
Sighing round my heart o'er the fond hopes that die;
Sighing like the night wind and sobbing like the rain,
Wailing for the lost one that comes not again;
Ah! I long for Jeanie and my heart bows low,
Never more to find her where the bright waters flow.

Funiculi, funicula

Words by: Edward Oxenford

Some think the world is
  made for fun and frolic
And so do I!
And so do I!
Some think it well to be
  all melancholic,
To pine and sigh.
To pine and sigh.
But I, I love to spend
  my time in singing
Some joyous song,
Some joyous song.
To set the air with music
  bravely ringing
Is far from wrong,
Is far from wrong!

Chorus:
Listen! Listen!
Echoes sound afar!
Listen! Listen!
Echoes sound afar!
Funiculi, funicula,
Funiculi, funicula!
Echoes sound afar!
Funiculi, funicula!

Some think it wrong to set
  the feet a-dancing.
But not so I!
But not so I!
Some think that eyes should
  keep coyly from glancing
Upon the sly,
Upon the sly.
But oh, to me the mazy
  dance is charming,
Divinely sweet,
Divinely sweet!
For surely there is nought
  that is alarming
In nimble feet,
In nimble feet!
(Chorus)

Home sweet home

Words by John Howard Payne

Ah, me! 'Tis strange that
   some should take to sighing
And like it well!
And like it well!
For me, I have not thought
   it worth the trying,
So cannot tell,
So cannot tell!
With laugh and dance and
   song the day soon passes,
Full soon is gone,
Full soon is gone!
For mirth was made for
   joyous lads and lasses
To call their own,
To call their own!
    (Chorus)

'Mid pleasures and palaces though I may roam,
Be it ever so humble, there's no place like home;
A charm from the sky seems to hallow us there,
Which, seek thro' the world, is ne'er met with elsewhere.

Chorus:
Home! Home! Sweet, sweet home!
There's no place like home,
There's no place like home.

An exile from home, splendor dazzles in vain,
Oh, give me my lowly thatched cottage again;
The birds singing gaily, that come at my call;
Give me them, with that peace of mind, dearer than all.
    (Chorus)

To thee, I'll return, overburdened with care,
The heart's dearest solace will smile on me there.
No more from that cottage again will I roam,
Be it ever so humble, there's no place like home.
    (Chorus)

Cockles and mussels

Traditional

In Dublin's fair city, where girls are so pretty,
I first set my eyes on sweet Molly Malone,
As she wheeled her wheelbarrow through streets broad
   and narrow,
Crying 'Cockles and mussels, alive, alive-o.'

Chorus:
Alive, alive-o, alive, alive-o,
Crying, 'Cockles and mussels, alive, alive-o.'

She was a fishmonger, but sure 'twas no wonder,
For so were her mother and father before,
And they each wheeled their barrow through streets
   broad and narrow,
Crying, 'Cockles and mussels, alive, alive-o.'
   (Chorus)

She died of a fever, and no one could save her,
And that was the end of sweet Molly Malone,
And her ghost wheeled her barrow through streets
   broad and narrow,
Crying, 'Cockles and mussels, alive, alive-o.'
   (Chorus)

Ta-ra-ra-Boom-der-é

Henry J. Sayers

A sweet Tuxedo girl you see,
   queen of swell society
Fond of fun as fond can be,
   when it's on the strict Q.T.
I'm not too young, I'm not too old,
   not too timid, not too bold,
Just the kind you'd like to hold,
   just the kind for sport, I'm told.

Chorus:
Ta-ra-ra Boom-der-é, Ta-ra-ra Boom-der-é,
Ta-ra-ra Boom-der-é, Ta-ra-ra Boom-der-é,
Ta-ra-ra Boom-der-é, Ta-ra-ra Boom-der-é,
Ta-ra-ra Boom-der-é, Ta-ra-ra Boom-der-é,

I'm a blushing bud of innocence,
   Papa says at big expense,
Old maids say I have no sense,
   boys declare I'm just immense;
Before my song I do conclude,
   I want it strictly understood,
Tho' fond of fun, I'm never rude,
   tho' not too bad, I'm not too good.
     (Chorus)

  Q.T.: quiet

Wouldn't it be loverly

Words by Alan Jay Lerner

From the show 'My Fair Lady'

All I want is a room somewhere,
Far away from the cold night air,
With one enormous chair;
Oh, wouldn't it be loverly?
Lots of choc'late for me to eat;
Lots of coal makin' lots of heat;
Warm face, warm hands, warm feet,
Oh, wouldn't it be loverly?
Oh, so loverly sittin' absobloomin'lutely still!
I would never budge 'til spring crept over the window sill.
Someone's head restin' on my knee;
Warm and tender as he can be;
Who takes good care of me.
Oh, wouldn't it be loverly?
Loverly! Loverly! Loverly! Loverly!

On Ilkla Moor baht 'at

Traditional Yorkshire

Wheear 'as tha bin sin' ah saw thee?
  On Ilkla Moor baht 'at.
Wheear 'as tha bin sin' ah saw thee?
Wheear 'as tha bin sin' ah saw thee?

Chorus:
On Ilkla Moor baht 'at.
On Ilkla Moor baht 'at.
On Ilkla Moor baht 'at.

Tha's bin a-coortin' Mary Jane
  On Ilkla Moor baht 'at.
Tha's bin a-coortin' Mary Jane.
Tha's bin a-coortin' Mary Jane.
  (Chorus)

Tha'll go an' get thi deearth o' cowld
  On Ilkla Moor baht 'at.
  (Repeat, as in first verse)
  (Chorus)

Then we shall ha' to bury thee
  On Ilkla Moor baht 'at.
  (Repeat, as in first verse)
  (Chorus)

Then t'worms'll coom an' ate thee oop
  On Ilkla Moor baht 'at.
  (Repeat, as in first verse)
  (Chorus)

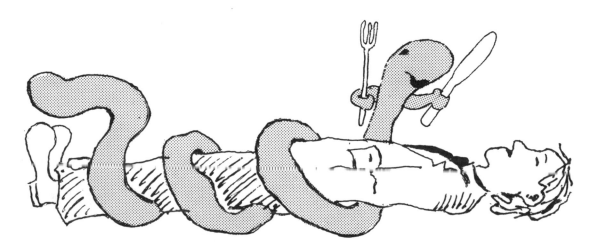

Then t'ducks'll coom an ate oop t'worms
  On Ilkla Moor baht 'at.
    (Repeat, as in first verse)
    (Chorus)

Then we shall go an' ate oop t'ducks
  On Ilkla Moor baht 'at.
    (Repeat, as in first verse)
    (Chorus)

Then we shall all 'av etten thee
  On Ilkla Moor baht 'at.
    (Repeat, as in first verse)
    (Chorus)

That's wheear we gets our oahn back
  On Ilkla Moor baht 'at.
    (Repeat, as in first verse)

baht 'at: without a hat

Early one morning

Early one morning, just as the sun was rising,
I heard a maiden singing in the valley below.
Oh, don't deceive me, Oh never leave me.
How can you use a poor maiden so?

Remember the vows that you made to me truly,
Remember how tenderly you nestled close to me.
Gay is the garland, fresh are the roses
I've culled from the garden, to bind over thee.

Here I now wander alone as I wonder
Why did you leave me to sigh and complain.
I ask of the roses, why should I be forsaken,
Why must I here in sorrow remain?

Through yonder grove by the spring that is running,
There you and I have so merrily played,
Kissing and courting and gently sporting,
Oh, my innocent heart you've betrayed.

How could you slight so pretty a girl who loves you,
A pretty girl who loves you so dearly and warm?
Though love's a folly is surely but a fancy,
Still it should prove to me sweeter than your scorn.

Soon you will meet with another pretty maiden,
Some pretty maid, you'll court her for a while;
Thus ever ranging, turning and changing,
Always seeking for a girl that is new.

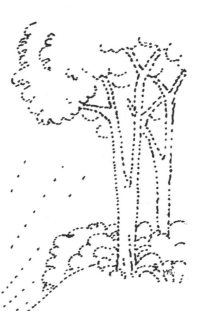

Green grow the rushes-ho

Traditional

I'll sing you one-ho!
Green grow the rushes ho.
What is your one-ho?
One is one and all alone and evermore shall be so.

I'll sing you two-ho!
Green grow the rushes ho.
What are your two-ho?
Two, two the lily-white boys, clothed all in green-ho,
One is one and all alone and evermore shall be so.

I'll sing you three-ho!
Green grow the rushes ho.
What are your three-ho?
Three, three the rivals,
Two, two the lily-white boys, clothed all in green-ho,
One is one and all alone and evermore shall be so.

I'll sing you four-ho!
Green grow the rushes ho.
What are your four-ho?
Four for the Gospel makers,
Three, three the rivals,
Two, two the lily-white boys, clothed all in green-ho,
One is one and all alone and evermore shall be so.

I'll sing you five-ho!
Green grow the rushes ho.
What are your five-ho?
Five for the symbols at your door
and four for the Gospel makers,
Three, three the rivals,
Two, two the lily-white boys, clothed all in green-ho,
One is one and all alone and evermore shall be so.

 I'll sing you six-ho!
Green grow the rushes ho.
What are your six-ho?
Six for the six proud walkers,
Five for the symbols at your door
and four for the Gospel makers,
Three, three the rivals,
Two, two the lily-white boys, clothed all in green-ho,
One is one and all alone and evermore shall be so.

I'll sing you seven-ho!
Green grow the rushes ho.
What are your seven-ho?
Seven for the seven stars in the sky
and six for the six proud walkers,
Five for the symbols at your door
and four for the Gospel makers,
Three, three the rivals,
Two, two the lily-white boys, clothed all in green-ho,
One is one and all alone and evermore shall be so.

 I'll sing you eight-ho!
Green grow the rushes ho.
What are your eight-ho?
Eight for the April rainers,
Seven for the seven stars in the sky
and six for the six proud walkers,
Five for the symbols at your door
and four for the Gospel makers,
Three, three the rivals,
Two, two the lily-white boys, clothed all in green-ho,
One is one and all alone and evermore shall be so.

I'll sing you nine-ho!
Green grow the rushes ho.
What are your nine-ho?
Nine for the nine bright shiners,
Eight for the April rainers,
Seven for the seven stars in the sky
and six for the six proud walkers,
Five for the symbols at your door
and four for the Gospel makers,
Three, three the rivals,
Two, two the lily-white boys, clothed all in green-ho,
One is one and all alone and evermore shall be so.

I'll sing you ten-ho!
Green grow the rushes ho.
What are your ten-ho?
Ten for the ten commandments,
Nine for the nine bright shiners,
Eight for the April rainers,
Seven for the seven stars in the sky
and six for the six proud walkers,
Five for the symbols at your door
and four for the Gospel makers,
Three, three the rivals,
Two, two the lily-white boys, clothed all in green-ho,
One is one and all alone and evermore shall be so.

I'll sing you eleven-ho!
Green grow the rushes ho.
What are your eleven-ho?
Eleven for the eleven went up to heaven
and ten for the ten commandments,
Nine for the nine bright shiners,
Eight for the April rainers,
Seven for the seven stars in the sky
and six for the six proud walkers,
Five for the symbols at your door
and four for the Gospel makers,
Three, three the rivals,
Two, two the lily-white boys, clothed all in green-ho,
One is one and all alone and evermore shall be so.

I'll sing you twelve-ho!
Green grow the rushes ho.
What are your twelve-ho?
Twelve for the twelve Apostles,
Eleven for the eleven went up to heaven
and ten for the ten commandments,
Nine for the nine bright shiners,
Eight for the April rainers,
Seven for the seven stars in the sky
and six for the six proud walkers,
Five for the symbols at your door
and four for the Gospel makers,
Three, three the rivals,
Two, two the lily-white boys, clothed all in green-ho,
One is one and all alone and evermore shall be so.

Greensleeves

Traditional English

Alas, my love! You do me wrong
To cast me off discourteously.
For I have loved you so long,
Delighting in your company.
Greensleeves was all my joy.
Greensleeves was my delight.
Greensleeves was my heart of gold,
And who but my lady Greensleeves?

My men were clothed all in green,
And they did ever attend on thee.
All this was gallant to be seen,
And yet, thou wouldst not love me.
Thou couldst desire no earthly thing,
But soon thou hadst it readily.
Thy music still I play and sing,
And yet thou wilt not love me.

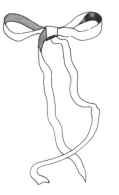

Oh, dear! what can the matter be?

Oh, dear! what can the matter be?
Oh, dear! what can the matter be?
Oh, dear! what can the matter be?
Johnny's so long at the fair.

He promised to buy me a basket of posies,
A garland of lilies, a garland of roses.
He promised to buy me a bunch of blue ribbons
To tie up my bonny brown hair.

Oh, dear! what can the matter be?
Oh, dear! what can the matter be?
Oh, dear! what can the matter be?
Johnny's so long at the fair.

Blow the man down

Traditional sea shanty

As I was a-walkin' down Paradise Street,
Singing way, hay, blow the man down,
A saucy young maiden I chanced for to meet.
Give me some time to blow the man down.

I asked, 'Where're you bound?'
   She said, 'Nowhere today,'
Singing way, hay, blow the man down,
'Now that's fine,' I replied,
   'For I'm headed that way.'
Give me some time to blow the man down.

We entered an ale-house looked down on the sea,
Singing way, hay, blow the man down,
There stood a policeman who stared right at me.
Give me some time to blow the man down.

Said he, 'You're a pirate that flies the black flag,
Singing way, hay, blow the man down,
You've robbed some poor Dutchmen and left them in rags.'
Give me some time to blow the man down.

'Oh, Officer, Officer, you do me wrong,
Singing way, hay, blow the man down,
I'm a freshwater sailor just in from Hong Kong.'
Give me some time to blow the man down.

But they jailed me six months in Old Lexington Town,
Singing way, hay, blow the man down,
For fighting and kicking and knocking him down.
Give me some time to blow the man down.

Come all you brave sailors who follow the sea,
Singing way, hay, blow the man down,
And join in a-singing this shanty with me!
Give me some time to blow the man down!

Skye boat song

Words by Sir Harold Boulton

'Speed, bonnie boat, like a bird on the wing,
Onward,' the sailors cry.
'Carry the lad that's born to be king
Over the sea to Skye.'

Loud the winds howl, loud the waves roar,
Thunder clouds rend the air;
Baffled, our foes stand on the shore,
Follow they will not dare.

'Speed, bonnie boat, like a bird on the wing,
Onward,' the sailors cry.
'Carry the lad that's born to be king
Over the sea to Skye.'

My bonnie lies over the ocean

Traditional North country

My bonnie lies over the ocean,
My bonnie lies over the sea,
My bonnie lies over the ocean,
O bring back my bonnie to me.

Chorus:
Bring back, bring back,
O bring back my bonnie to me, to me.
Bring back, bring back,
O bring back my bonnie to me.

Last night as I lay on my pillow,
Last night as I lay on my bed,
Last night as I lay on my pillow,
I dreamed that my bonnie was dead.
　　(Chorus)

O blow ye winds over the ocean,
O blow ye winds over the sea,
O blow ye winds over the ocean,
And bring back my bonnie to me.
　　(Chorus)

The winds have blown over the ocean,
The winds have blown over the sea,
The winds have blown over the ocean,
And brought back my bonnie to me.
　　(Chorus)

Widdicombe Fair

Traditional West country

Tom Pearce, Tom Pearce lend me your gray mare,
   All along, down along, out along lee.
For I want for to go to Widdicombe Fair

    Chorus:
    With Bill Brewer, Jan Stewer,
    Peter Gurney, Peter Davy,
    Dan'l Whiddon, Harry Hawk,
    Old Uncle Tom Cobbleigh and all,
    Old Uncle Tom Cobbleigh and all.

     And when shall I see again my gray mare?
      All along, down along, out along lee.
     By Friday soon, or Saturday noon,
        (Chorus)

       So they harnessed and bridled the old gray mare,
        All along, down along, out along lee
      And off they drove to Widdicombe Fair,
         (Chorus)

        Then Friday came and Saturday noon,
         All along, down along, out along lee.
        But Tom Pearce's old mare have not trotted home,
          (Chorus)

So Tom Pearce he got up to the top of the hill,
  All along, down along, out along lee.
And he seed his old mare down a-making her will,
    (Chorus)

    So Tom Pearce's old mare her took sick and died
      All along, down along, out along lee
    And Tom he sat down on a stone and he cried,
        (Chorus)

    But this isn't the end of this shocking affair,
      All along, down along, out along lee.
    Nor, though they be dead, of the horrid career,
        (Chorus)

    When the wind whistles cold on the moor of a night,
      All along, down along, out along lee.
    Tom Pearce's old mare does appear ghastly white,
        (Chorus)

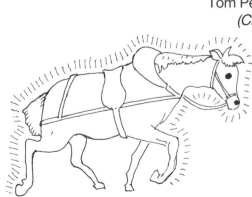

    And all the night long be heard skirling and groans,
      All along, down along, out along lee.
    From Tom Pearce's old mare and a rattling of bones,
        (Chorus)

What shall we do with a drunken sailor?

What shall we do with a drunken sailor?
What shall we do with a drunken sailor?
What shall we do with a drunken sailor?
Early in the morning.

Chorus:
Way, hey and up she rises,
Way, hey and up she rises,
Way, hey and up she rises,
Early in the morning.

Put him in the longboat till he's sober,
Put him in the longboat till he's sober,
Put him in the longboat till he's sober,
Early in the morning.
    (Chorus)

Pull out the plug and wet him all over,
Pull out the plug and wet him all over,
Pull out the plug and wet him all over,
Early in the morning.
    (Chorus)

Put him in the scuppers with a hose pipe on him,
Put him in the scuppers with a hose pipe on him,
Put him in the scuppers with a hose pipe on him,
Early in the morning.
    (Chorus)

Heave him by the leg in a running bowline,
Heave him by the leg in a running bowline,
Heave him by the leg in a running bowline,
Early in the morning.
(Chorus)

Shave his belly with a rusty razor,
Shave his belly with a rusty razor,
Shave his belly with a rusty razor,
Early in the morning.
(Chorus)

Shenandoah

Oh, Shenandoah, I love your daughter.
Away, you rolling river.
I'll take her cross yonder water.

Chorus:
Away, we're bound away.
'Cross the wide Missouri.

Oh, Shenandoah, she took my fancy.
Away, you rolling river.
Oh, Shenandoah, I love your Nancy.
(Chorus)

Oh, Shenandoah, I long to see you.
Away, you rolling river.
Oh, Shenandoah, I'm drawing near you.
(Chorus)

Oh, Shenandoah, I'm bound to leave you.
Away, you rolling river.
Oh, Shenandoah, I'll ne'er deceive you.
(Chorus)

Oh, Shenandoah, I'll ne'er forget you.
Away, you rolling river.
Oh, Shenandoah, I'll ever love you.
(Chorus)

Sur le pont d'Avignon

Sur le pont d'Avignon,
L'on y danse, l'on y danse,
Sur le pont d'Avignon,
L'on y danse tout en rond!

    Les beaux messieurs font comm' ci,
    Et puis encor' comm' ca.

        Les belles dam's font comm' ci,
        Et puis encor' comm' ca.

            Les militair's font comm' ci,
            Et puis encor' comm' ca.

On the bridge at Avignon,
See them dancing, see them dancing,
On the bridge at Avignon,
See them dancing round and round!

    Gentlemen bow this way,
    Then again bow that way.

        Ladies all bow this way,
        Then again bow that way.

            Soldiers, they bow this way,
            Then again bow that way.

Alouette

French folk song

Alouette, gentille Alouette,
Alouette, je te plumerai.
Je te plumerai le bec,
Je te plumerai le bec.
Et le bec, et le bec,
Et la tête, et la tête,

Alouette, gentille Alouette,
Alouette, je te plumerai.
Je te plumerai les yeux,
Je te plumerai les yeux,
Et les yeux, et les yeux,
Et le bec, et le bec,
Et la tête, et la tête,

Alouette, gentille Alouette,
Alouette, je te plumerai.
Je te plumerai les ailes,
Je te plumerai les ailes,
Et les ailes, et les ailes,
Et les yeux, et les yeux,
Et le bec, et le bec,
Et la tête, et la tête,

Alouette, gentille Alouette,
Alouette, je te plumerai.
Je te plumerai le dos,
Je te plumerai le dos,
Et le dos, et le dos,
Et les ailes, et les ailes,
Et les yeux, et les yeux,
Et le bec, et le bec,
Et la tête, et la tête,

Alouette, gentille Alouette,
Alouette, je te plumerai.
Je te plumerai les jambes,
Je te plumerai les jambes,
Et les jambes, et les jambes,
Et le dos, et le dos,
Et les ailes, et les ailes,
Et les yeux, et les yeux,
Et le bec, et le bec,
Et la tête, et la tête,

Alouette, gentille Alouette,
Alouette, je te plumerai.
Je te plumerai les pieds
Je te plumerai les pieds
Et les pieds, et les pieds,
Et les jambes, et les jambes,
Et le dos, et le dos,
Et les ailes, et les ailes,
Et les yeux, et les yeux,
Et le bec, et le bec,
Et la tête, et la tête,
Aloutte, gentille Alouette,
Alouette, je te plumerai.

alouette: lark

Frère Jacques

Traditional French

Frère Jacques, Frère Jacques,
Dormez-vous? Dormez-vous?
Sonnez les matines, Sonnez les matines,
Din, din, don! Din, din, don!

Traditional English translation:

Brother John, Brother John,
Are you sleeping? Are you sleeping?
Morning bells are ringing,
Morning bells are ringing,
Ding, dong, ding! Ding, dong, ding!

I belong to Glasgow

Words & music by Will Fyffe

I've been wi' a few o' ma cronies,
One or two pals o' ma ain.
We went in a hotel, where we did very well,
And then we came out once again.
Then we went into another,
And that is the reason I'm fou,
We had six deoch an' dorises, then sang a chorus,
Just listen, I'll sing it to you.

Chorus:
I belong to Glasgow, dear old Glasgow town!
But what's the matter wi' Glasgow?
For it's going round and round.
I'm only a common old working chap,
As anyone can see,
But when I get a couple of drinks on a Saturday,
Glasgow belongs to me.

There's nothing in being teetotal,
And saving a shilling or two.
If your money you spend, you've nothing to lend;
Well, that's all the better for you.
There's nae harm in taking a drappie,
It ends all your trouble and strife,
It gives you the feeling, that when you get home
You don't care a hang for the wife.
      (Chorus)

deoch an' dorises: parting drinks
a drappie: little drop

I do like to be beside the seaside

Words by John A. Glover-Kind

Oh! I do like to be beside the seaside,
I do like to be beside the sea.
I do like to stroll upon the
    Prom, Prom, Prom,
Where the brass bands play
    Tiddely-om-pom-pom!
So just let me be beside the seaside,
I'll be beside myself with glee;
And there's lots of girls besides
I should like to be beside,
Beside the seaside, beside the sea.

Little brown jug

Words by 'Eastburn' Joseph E. Winner

My wife and I lived all alone,
In a little log hut
   we called our own.
She loved gin,
   and I loved rum.
I tell you what,
   we'd lots of fun!

Chorus:
Ha, ha, ha, you and me,
Little brown jug,
   don't I love thee.
Ha, ha, ha, you and me,
Little brown jug,
   don't I love thee.

'Tis you who makes
   my friends my foes
'Tis you who makes me
   wear old clothes,
Here you are,
   so near my nose,
So tip her up,
   and down she goes.
   (Chorus)

When I go toiling
   to my farm,
I take little brown jug
   under my arm.
I place it under a shady tree.
Little brown jug,
   'tis you and me.
   (Chorus)

If all the folks in Adam's race
Were gathered together
   in one place,
Then I'd prepare
   to shed a tear
Before I'd part from you,
   my dear.
   (Chorus)

If I'd a cow that
   gave such milk,
I'd clothe her in
   the finest silk.
I'd feed her on
   the choicest hay.
And milk her forty
   times a day.
   (Chorus)

The rose is red;
   my nose is, too.
The violet's blue,
   and so are you.
And yet I guess before I stop,
We'd better take
   another drop.
   (Chorus)

My grandfather's clock

Words by Henry C. Work

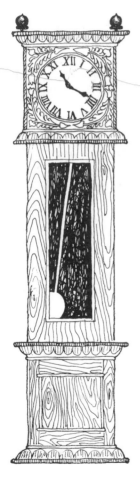

My grandfather's clock was too large for the shelf,
So it stood ninety years on the floor.
It was taller by half than the old man himself,
Though it weighed not a pennyweight more.
It was bought on the morn of the day that he was born,
And was always his treasure and pride –

Chorus:
But it stopped short, never to go again,
When the old man died.
Ninety years without slumbering,
Tick, tock, tick, tock,
His life seconds numbering,
Tick, tock, tick, tock.
It stopped short, never to go again,
When the old man died.

In watching its pendulum swing to and fro,
Many hours he spent while a boy;
And in childhood and manhood, the clock seemed to know
And to share both his grief and his joy.
For it struck twenty-four when he entered at the door
With a blooming and beautiful bride –
    (Chorus)

It rang an alarm in the dead of the night,
An alarm that for years had been dumb;
And we knew that his spirit was pluming for flight,
That his hour of departure had come.
Still the clock kept the time, with a soft and muffled chime
As we silently stood by its side –
    (Chorus)

Lavender's blue

Lavender's blue, diddle, diddle,
   Lavender's green;
When I am king, diddle, diddle,
   You shall be queen.

Call up your men, diddle, diddle,
   Set them to work;
Some to the plough, diddle, diddle,
   Some to the fork.

Some to make hay, diddle, diddle,
   Some to cut corn;
While you and I, diddle, diddle,
   Keep ourselves warm.

Roll out the barrel

Words by Lew Brown, Wladimir A. Timm and Jaromir Vejvoda

Every time they hear that oom-pa-pa,
Everybody feels so tra-la-la,
They want to throw their cares away,
They all go lah-de-ah-de-ay,
Then they hear a rumble on the floor,
It's the big surprise they're waiting for,
And all the couples form a ring;
For miles around you'll hear them sing:

Chorus:
Roll out the barrel,
We'll have a barrel of fun.
Roll out the barrel,
We've got the blues on the run.
Zing! Boom! Ta-rarrel!
Ring out a song of good cheer.
Now's the time to roll the barrel,
For the gang's all here!

Island in the sun

Words by Harry Belafonte and Lord Burgess (Irving Burgie)

This is my island in the sun
Where my people have toiled since time begun;
'Though I may sail on many a sea,
Her shores will always be home to me.

Chorus:
Oh, island in the sun,
Willed to me by my father's hand,
All my days I will sing in praise
Of your forests, waters, your shining sand.

When morning breaks the heaven on high,
I lift my heavy load to the sky;
Sun comes down with a burning glow
That mingles my sweat with the earth below.
(Chorus)

I see woman on bended knee,
Cutting cane for her family.
I see man at the waterside,
Casting nets at the surging tide.
(Chorus)

I hope the day will never come
That I can't awake to the sound of drum.
Never let me miss carnival
With calypso songs philosophical.
(Chorus)

The happy wanderer

Words by Antonia Ridge

I love to go a-wandering
Along the mountain track,
And as I go, I love to sing,
My knapsack on my back.
　Val-de ri, Val-de ra,
　Val-de ra,
　Val-de ha ha ha ha ha ha,
　Val-de ri, Val-de ra,
My knapsack on my back.

I love to wander by the stream
That dances in the sun.
So joyously it calls to me,
'Come! Join my happy song!'
　Val-de ri, Val-de ra,
　Val-de ra,
　Val-de ha ha ha ha ha ha,
　Val-de ri, Val-de ra,
'Come! Join my happy song!'

I wave my hat to all I meet
And they wave back to me,
And blackbirds call so loud and sweet
From every greenwood tree.
　Val-de ri, Val-de ra,
　Val-de ra,
　Val-de ha ha ha ha ha ha,
　Val-de ri, Val-de ra,
From every greenwood tree.

High overhead, the skylarks wing,
They never rest at home,
But just like me, they love to sing,
As o'er the world we roam.
　Val-de ri, Val-de ra,
　Val-de ra,
　Val-de ha ha ha ha ha ha,
　Val-de ri, Val-de ra,
As o'er the world we roam.

Oh, may I go a-wandering
Until the day I die!
Oh, may I always laugh and sing
Beneath God's clear blue sky!
　Val-de ri, Val-de ra,
　Val-de ra,
　Val-de ha ha ha ha ha ha,
　Val-de ri, Val-de ra,
Beneath God's clear blue sky!

Annie Laurie

Maxwelton's braes are bonnie,
Where early fa's the dew,
And it's there that Annie Laurie
Gave me her promise true,
Gave me her promise true,
Which ne'er forgot will be;
And for bonnie Annie Laurie
I'd lay me doon an' dee.

Her brow is like the snawdrift,
Her neck is like the swan,
Her face it is the fairest
That e'er the sun shone on,
That e'er the sun shone on,
An' dark blue is her ee,
And for bonnie Annie Laurie
I'd lay me doon an' dee.

Like dew on the gowan lying
Is the fa' o' her fairy feet;
An' like winds in summer sighing,
Her voice is low an' sweet,
Her voice is low an' sweet,
An' she's a' the world to me,
And for bonnie Annie Laurie
I'd lay me doon an' dee.

So long, it's been good to know you

Words by Woody Guthrie

I've sung this song, but I'll sing it again,
Of the people I've met and the places I've seen,
Of some of the troubles that bothered my mind,
And a lot of good people that I've left behind.
   saying:

Chorus:
So long, it's been good to know you,
So long, it's been good to know you,
So long, it's been good to know you.
What a long time since I've been home,
And I gotta be driftin' along.

The sweethearts they sat in the dark and they sparked,
They hugged and they kissed in that dusty old dark,
They sighed and they cried and they hugged and they kissed,
But instead of marriage, they talked like this,
   Honey:
     (Chorus)

I went to your family and asked them for you.
They all said, 'Take her, oh take her, please do!
She can't cook or sew and she won't scrub your floor.'
So I put on my hat and tiptoed out the door,
   saying:
     (Chorus)

Down by the riverside

Traditional spiritual

Going to lay down my sword and shield,
Down by the riverside,
Down by the riverside,
Down by the riverside.
Going to lay down my sword and shield,
Down by the riverside,
Down by the riverside.

Chorus:
I ain't going to study war no more,
I ain't going to study war no more,
I ain't going to study war no more,
I ain't going to study war no more,
I ain't going to study war no more,
Down by the riverside.

Going to lay down my heavy load,
Down by the riverside,
    (Repeat as above, followed by chorus)

Going to ride on a milk-white horse,
Down by the riverside,
    (Repeat as above, followed by chorus)

Going to try on a snow-white robe,
Down by the riverside,
    (Repeat as above, followed by chorus)

Going to put on my starry crown,
Down by the riverside,
    (Repeat as above, followed by chorus)

Getting ready to meet my Lord,
Down by the riverside,
    (Repeat as above, followed by chorus)

Swing low, sweet chariot

Spiritual

I looked over Jordan and what did I see,
    Comin' for to carry me home?
A band of angels comin' after me,
    Comin' for to carry me home.

Chorus:
Swing low, sweet chariot,
    Comin' for to carry me home,
Swing low, sweet chariot,
    Comin' for to carry me home.

If you get there before I do,
    Comin' for to carry me home.
Tell all my friends I'm comin' too,
    Comin' for to carry me home.
        (Chorus)

The brightest day that I ever saw,
    Comin' for to carry me home.
When Jesus washed my sins away,
    Comin' for to carry me home.
        (Chorus)

I'm sometimes up and sometimes down,
    Comin' for to carry me home.
But still my soul feels heavenly bound,
    Comin' for to carry me home.
        (Chorus)

Joshua fought the battle of Jericho

Traditional spiritual

Chorus:
Joshua fought the battle of Jericho,
Jericho, Jericho –
Joshua fought the battle of Jericho,
And the walls came tumbling down.

You may talk about your kings of Gideon,
You may talk about your men of Saul,
But there's none like good old Josh-u-ay
At the battle of Jericho (that morning.)
    (Chorus)

Up to the walls of Jericho
He marched with spear in hand,
'Go blow those ram-horns,' Joshua cried,
'Cause the battle is in my hands.'
    (Chorus)

Then the lamb ram sheephorns began to blow,
The trumpets began to sound.
Joshua commanded the children to shout,
And the walls come a-tumbling down.
    (Chorus)

There's no man like Joshua
No man like Saul
No man like Joshua
At the battle of Jericho.
    (Chorus)

He's got the whole world in His hands

Traditional spiritual

He's got the whole world in His hands.
He's got the whole wide world in His hands.
He's got the whole world in His hands.

Chorus:
He's got the whole world in His hands.

He's got the wind and the rain in His hands.
He's got the wind and the rain in His hands.
He's got the wind and the rain in His hands.
    (Chorus)

He's got the little tiny baby in His hands.
He's got the little tiny baby in His hands.
He's got the little tiny baby in His hands.
    (Chorus)

He's got you and me, brother, in His hands.
He's got you and me, brother, in His hands.
He's got you and me, sister, in His hands.
    (Chorus)

He's got the Sun and the Moon in His hands.
He's got the Sun and the Moon in His hands.
He's got the Moon and the stars in His hands.
    (Chorus)

He's got love and salvation in His hands.
He's got love and salvation in His hands.
He's got love and salvation in His hands.
(Chorus)

He's got everybody here in His hands.
He's got everybody here in His hands.
He's got everybody here in His hands.
(Chorus)

Michael, row the boat ashore

Chorus:
Michael, row the boat ashore,
   Hallelujah.
Michael, row the boat ashore,
   Hallelujah.

Sister, help to trim the sail,
   Hallelujah.
Sister, help to trim the sail,
   Hallelujah.
     (Chorus)

Brother, won't you give a hand?
   Hallelujah.
Steer this boat to the Promised Land,
   Hallelujah.
     (Chorus)

Jordan's deep and Jordan's wide,
   Hallelujah.
Milk and honey the other side,
   Hallelujah.
     (Chorus)

Dry bones

Spiritual

Dem bones, dem bones, dem dry bones
Dem bones, dem bones, dem dry bones
Dem bones, dem bones, dem dry bones
Now hear the word of the Lord!

The toe bone's connected to the foot bone
The foot bone's connected to the ankle bone
The ankle bone's connected to the leg bone
Now hear the word of the Lord!

The leg bone's connected to the thigh bone
The thigh bone's connected to the hip bone
The hip bone's connected to the back bone
Now hear the word of the Lord!

The back bone's connected to the shoulder bone
The shoulder bone's connected to the neck bone
The neck bone's connected to the head bone
Now hear the word of the Lord!

Dem bones, dem bones gonna walk around
Dem bones, dem bones gonna walk around
Dem bones, dem bones gonna walk around
Now hear the word of the Lord!

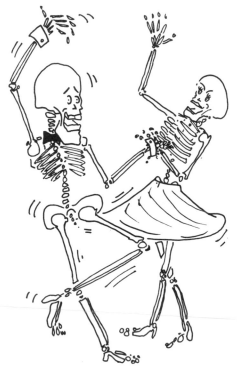

When the saints go marching in

Spiritual

I am just a lonely traveller
Through this big wide world of sin,
Want to join that grand procession
When the saints go marching in.

Chorus:
Oh, when the saints go marching in,
Oh, when the saints go marching in,
Lord, I want to be in that number
When the saints go marching in.

Come and join me on my journey,
'Cause it's time we did begin,
And we'll be there for that judgement
When the saints go marching in.
(Chorus)

We are marching in the footsteps
Of those who've marched before,
And someday we'll be united,
When we meet those saints once more.
(Chorus)

O Sinner Man

Spiritual

Chorus:
O sinner man, where you going to run to?
O sinner man, where you going to run to?
O sinner man, where you going to run to?
All on that day.

Run to the sun, O sun won't you hide me?
Run to the sun, O sun won't you hide me?
Run to the sun, O sun won't you hide me?
All on that day.

The Lord said, O sinner man the sun'll be a burning
The Lord said, O sinner man the sun'll be a burning
The Lord said, O sinner man the sun'll be a burning
All on that day.
    (Chorus)

Run to the moon, O moon won't you hide me? *(three times)*
All on that day.

The Lord said, O sinner man the moon'll be a bleeding *(three times)*
All on that day.
    (Chorus)

Run to the stars, O stars won't you hide me? *(three times)*
All on that day.

The Lord said, O sinner man the stars'll be a falling *(three times)*
All on that day.
    (Chorus)

Run to the sea, O sea won't you hide me? *(three times)*
All on that day.

The Lord said, O sinner man the sea'll be a sinking *(three times)*
All on that day.
 (Chorus)

Run to the rocks, O rocks won't you hide me? *(three times)*
All on that day.

The Lord said, O sinner man the rocks'll be a rolling *(three times)*
All on that day.
 (Chorus)

Run to the Lord, O Lord won't you hide me? *(three times)*
All on that day.

The Lord said, O sinner man you ought to be a praying *(three times)*
All on that day.
 (Chorus)

Sinner man says, Lord I've been a praying *(three times)*
All on that day.

The Lord said, O sinner man you prayed too late *(three times)*
All on that day.
 (Chorus)

Run to Satan, O Satan won't you hide me? *(three times)*
All on that day.

Satan said, O sinner man step right in *(three times)*
All on that day.
 (Chorus)

The Yellow Rose of Texas

Words by 'J.K.'

There's a Yellow Rose in Texas
That I am going to see
No other fellow knows her
No, not a one but me.
She cried so when I left her
It like to broke my heart.
And if I ever find her
We never more will part.

Chorus:
She's the sweetest rose in Texas
That this man ever knew.
Her eyes are bright as diamonds:
They sparkle like the dew.
You may talk about your dearest May
And sing of Rosa Lee,
But the Yellow Rose of Texas
Beats the belles of Tennessee.

Where the Rio Grande is flowing
And starry skies are bright,
She walks along the river
In the quiet summer night.
She asks if I remember
When we parted long ago,
I promised to come back again,
And not to leave her so.
(Chorus)

Oh, now I'm going to find her
For my heart is full of woe.
We'll sing the songs together
We sung so long ago.
We'll play the banjo gaily,
We'll sing the songs of yore,
And the Yellow Rose of Texas
Will be mine forevermore.
(Chorus)

When Johnny comes marching home again

Words by Louis Lambert

When Johnny comes marching home again,
   Hurrah! Hurrah!
We'll give him a hearty welcome then,
   Hurrah! Hurrah!
The men will cheer, the boys will shout,
The ladies they will all turn out.

Chorus:
And we'll all feel gay when
Johnny comes marching home.
And we'll all feel gay when
Johnny comes marching home.

The old church bell will peal with joy
   Hurrah! Hurrah!
To welcome home our darling boy.
   Hurrah! Hurrah!
The village lads and lassies say
With roses they will strew the way.
   (Chorus)

Get ready for the Jubilee.
   Hurrah! Hurrah!
We'll give the hero three times three.
   Hurrah! Hurrah!
The laurel wreath is ready now
To place upon his loyal brow.   *(Chorus)*

Let love and friendship on that day
   Hurrah! Hurrah!
Their choicest treasures then display.
   Hurrah! Hurrah!
And let each one perform some part
To fill with joy his warriors' heart.
   (Chorus)

My darling Clementine

Words by Percy Montrose

In a cavern, in a canyon
Excavating for a mine
Dwelt a miner, Forty-Niner
And his daughter,
    Clementine.

Chorus:
Oh, my darling,
    oh my darling,
Oh, my darling Clementine.
You are lost and
    gone forever –
Dreadful sorry, Clementine!

Light she was, and
    like a fairy,
And her shoes
    were number nine.
Herring boxes
    without topses,
Sandals were for Clementine.
    (Chorus)

Drove she ducklings to
    the water
Every morning just at nine.
Struck her toe against
    a splinter,
Fell into the foaming brine.
    (Chorus)

Ruby lips above the water
Blowing bubbles
    soft and fine.
Woe is me, I was
    no swimmer,
So I lost my Clementine.
    (Chorus)

Then the miner, Forty-Niner
He grew sad, began to pine,
Thought he oughter
    'jine' his daughter.
Now he's gone – like
    Clementine.

Forty-niner: miner in the 1849 Californian gold rush

Home on the range

Traditional Cowboy American

Oh, give me a home where the buffalo roam,
Where the deer and the antelope play,
Where seldom is heard a discouraging word,
And the sky is not clouded all day.

Chorus:
Home, home on the range!
Where the deer and the antelope play.
Where seldom is heard
A discouraging word,
And the sky is not clouded all day.

Oh, give me a gale
    on some soft Southern vale,
Where the stream of life joyfully flows,
On the banks of the river,
    where seldom if ever,
Any poisonous herbiage grows.
    (Chorus)

Oh, give me a land where the bright
    diamond sands
Lie awash in the glittering stream,
Where days glide along in leisure and song,
And afternoons pass as a dream.
    (Chorus)

I love the bright flowers in this frontier of ours,
And I thrill to the eagle's shrill scream.
Blood red are the rocks,
     brown the antelope flocks
That browse on the prairie so green.
          (Chorus)

The breezes are pure, and the sky is azure,
And the zephyrs so balmy and slow,
That I would not exchange
     my home on the range
For a townhouse in San Francisco.
          (Chorus)

How often at night,
     when the heavens are bright
With the light of the unclouded stars,
Have I stood here amazed
     and asked, as I gazed,
If their glory exceeds that of ours.
          (Chorus)

On top of old Smoky

Traditional Appalachian

Chorus:
On top of old Smoky,
All covered with snow,
I lost my true lover
From a-courtin' too slow.

On top of old Smoky
I went for a weep,
For a false-hearted lover
Is worse than a thief.
          (Chorus optional)

For a thief, he will rob you
Of all that you have,
But a false-hearted lover
Will send you to your grave.
          (Chorus optional)

He'll hug you and kiss you
And tell you more lies
Than the ties of the railroad
Or the stars in the skies.

John Brown's body

Words by Charles S. Hall

John Brown's body lies
   a-mouldering in the grave,
John Brown's body lies
   a-mouldering in the grave,
John Brown's body lies
   a-mouldering in the grave,
His soul goes marching on!

Chorus:
Glory, glory hallelujah!
Glory, glory hallelujah!
Glory, glory hallelujah!
His soul goes marching on!

Stars in Heaven are all
   looking kindly down,
Stars in Heaven are all
   looking kindly down,
Stars in Heaven are all
   looking kindly down,
His soul goes marching on!
   (Chorus)

John Brown's knapsack is
   strapped upon his back,
John Brown's knapsack is
   strapped upon his back,
John Brown's knapsack is
   strapped upon his back,
His soul goes marching on!
   (Chorus)

He's gone to be a soldier
   in the army of the Lord,
He's gone to be a soldier
   in the army of the Lord,
He's gone to be a soldier
   in the army of the Lord,
His soul goes marching on!
   (Chorus)

John Brown: American abolitionist

Jingle bells

J.S. Pierpont

Dashing through the snow
In a one-horse open sleigh,
O'er the fields we go,
Laughing all the way;
Bells on bob-tail ring,
Making spirits bright;
What fun it is to ride and sing
A sleighing song tonight!

Chorus:
Jingle bells! Jingle bells!
Jingle all the way!
Oh what fun it is to ride
In a one-horse open sleigh.
Oh! Jingle bells! Jingle bells!
Jingle all the way!
Oh what fun it is to ride
In a one-horse open sleigh.

A day or two ago
I thought I'd take a ride
And soon Miss Fannie Bright
Was seated by my side;
The horse was lean and lank,
Misfortune seem'd his lot,
He got into a drifted bank,
And then we got upsot!
(Chorus)

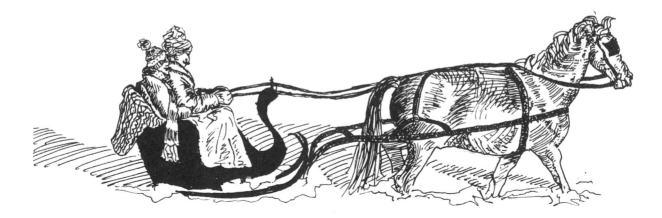

The twelve days of Christmas

On the first day of Christmas my true love gave to me
   A partridge in a pear tree.

On the second day of Christmas my true love gave to me
Two turtle doves
   And a partridge in a pear tree.

On the third day of Christmas my true love gave to me
Three French hens, two turtle doves
   And a partridge in a pear tree.

On the fourth day of Christmas my true love gave to me
Four colly birds, three French hens, two turtle doves
   And a partridge in a pear tree.

On the fifth day of Christmas my true love gave to me
Five golden rings, four colly birds, three French hens,
   two turtle doves
   And a partridge in a pear tree.

On the sixth day of Christmas my true love gave to me
Six geese a-laying, five golden rings, four colly birds,
   three French hens, two turtle doves
   And a partridge in a pear tree.

On the seventh day of Christmas my true love gave to me
Seven swans a-swimming, six geese a-laying, five golden rings,
   four colly birds, three French hens, two turtle doves
   And a partridge in a pear tree.

On the eighth day of Christmas my true love gave to me
Eight maids a-milking, seven swans a-swimming, six geese
   a-laying, five golden rings, four colly birds, three
   French hens, two turtle doves
   And a partridge in a pear tree.

On the ninth day of Christmas my true love gave to me
Nine ladies dancing, eight maids a-milking, seven swans
   a-swimming, six geese a-laying, five golden rings,
   four colly birds, three French hens, two turtle doves
   And a partridge in a pear tree.

On the tenth day of Christmas my true love gave to me
Ten lords a-leaping, nine ladies dancing, eight maids a-milking,
   seven swans a-swimming, six geese a-laying, five golden rings,
   four colly birds, three French hens, two turtle doves
   And a partridge in a pear tree.

On the eleventh day of Christmas my true love gave to me
Eleven pipers playing, ten lords a-leaping, nine ladies
   dancing, eight maids a-milking, seven swans a-swimming,
   six geese a-laying, five golden rings, four colly birds,
   three French hens, two turtle doves
   And a partridge in a pear tree.

On the twelfth day of Christmas my true love gave to me
Twelve drummers drumming, eleven pipers playing,
   ten lords a-leaping, nine ladies dancing, eight maids
   a-milking, seven swans a-swimming, six geese a-laying,
   five golden rings, four colly birds, three French hens,
   two turtle doves
   And a partridge in a pear tree.

colly birds: blackbirds

Rudolph the red-nosed reindeer

Words & Music by Johnny Marks

Rudolph the red-nosed reindeer had a very shiny nose;
And if you ever saw it, you would even say it glows.
All of the other reindeer used to laugh and call him names;
They never let poor Rudolph join in any reindeer games.
Then one foggy Christmas Eve, Santa came to say:
'Rudolph, with your nose so bright, won't you guide my
   sleigh tonight?'
Then how the reindeer loved him as they shouted out with glee:
'Rudolph, the red-nosed reindeer, you'll go down in history.'

Go tell it on the mountain

When I was a learner,
I sought both night and day,
I asked the Lord to help me,
And He showed me the way.

Chorus:
Go tell it on the mountain;
Over the hills and ev'rywhere;
Go tell it on the mountain,
Our Jesus Christ is born.

While shepherds kept their watching;
O'er wand'ring flock by night;
Behold! From out the Heavens,
There shone a holy light.
(Chorus)

He made me a watchman
Upon the city wall,
And if I am a Christian
I am the least of all.
(Chorus)

And, lo, when they had seen it,
They all bowed down and prayed;
Then travelled on together,
To where the Babe was laid.
(Chorus)

Ding dong merrily on high

Ding dong! merrily on high
in heav'n the bells are ringing:
Ding dong! verily the sky
is riv'n with Angels singing.
Gloria,
Hosanna in excelsis.

E'en so here below, below
let steeple bells be swungen,
And i-o, i-o, i-o
by priest and people sungen.
Gloria,
Hosanna in excelsis.

Pray you, dutifully prime
your matin chime, ye ringers;
May you beautifully rime
your evetime song, ye singers:
Gloria,
Hosanna in excelsis.

Acknowledgments

Other interesting books from Exley:

In the same series

Free Stuff for Kids. £3.50 (paperback). This is a super book for children from six to eleven. It contains over 250 special offers of posters, badges, books, games and crafts which children can send off for, all either free or very cheap. They can write to Kodak, the Pony Club, Stanley Gibbons, Nestle, Lloyds Bank, the Nature Conservancy Council and dozens of other organizations. The book is extremely educational. Children love receiving letters and, once they've got this book, they wait for the post with enormous excitement!

Rainy Day Fun and Games. £3.50 (paperback). With over 100 things to make or do, children will actually look forward to a rainy day with this book in the house. There are so many different ideas; why not grow your own plants indoors, make something delicious to eat, build a landscape for your dinosaurs, puzzle your friends with some magic, or try one of the many card or party games. You need't wait for the rain to start having fun.

Play As We Go. £3.50 (paperback). Most parents dread taking children on long journeys because of the boredom factor. However, with this book to hand, this should never be a problem again! Packed with games and small-scale activities for children ranging from three to thirteen, this should keep them amused for hours and prevent fraying tempers all round.

Other Titles:
Crafty Ideas From Nature. £4.99 (hardback). This popular book for young children stresses "learning by doing" – and having fun at the same time. Packed full of good ideas for things to make and do using natural products, there are over 40 projects ranging from making floral notepaper, through jewellery and presents, to growing a miniature garden and some fun board games. Illustrated throughout in full colour and with step-by-step instructions, all these projects have been tried out by parents and teachers of children in the first years at school. This book has been authored by Myrna Daitz and Shirley Williams, while Gillian Chapman has illustrated several top-selling early-learning books.

Also in this exciting series: **Crafty Ideas From Junk, Crafty Ideas For Presents, Crafty Ideas For Parties** and new in 1991 **Crafty Ideas For Science.**

PEOPLE WHO HAVE HELPED THE WORLD: This important series of biographies for children aged eleven to fourteen has been acclaimed as one of the best biography series to have been produced for years. Illustrated throughout in colour and black-and-white and hardback, they cost £5.99 each.

Titles published or in preparation include: **Robert Baden Powell/Louis Braille/Marie Curie/ The Dalai Lama/Father Damien/Henry Dunant/Mahatma Gandhi/ Bob Geldof/Mikhail Gorbachev/Martin Luther King/ Maria Montessori/Florence Nightingale/Louis Pasteur/ Sir Peter Scott/Albert Schweitzer/Mother Teresa/ Desmond Tutu/Lech Walesa/Raoul Wallenberg**

These books can be ordered from your local bookseller or from Exley Publications Ltd, 16 Chalk Hill, Watford, Herts WD1 4BN. (Please send £1.50 to cover post and packing for 1 book, £2.25 for 2 or more books). Exley Publications reserves the right to show new retail prices on books which may vary from those previously advertised.